THE NOISE OF THE RAIN

COLLECTED POEMS

SARAH PLIMPTON

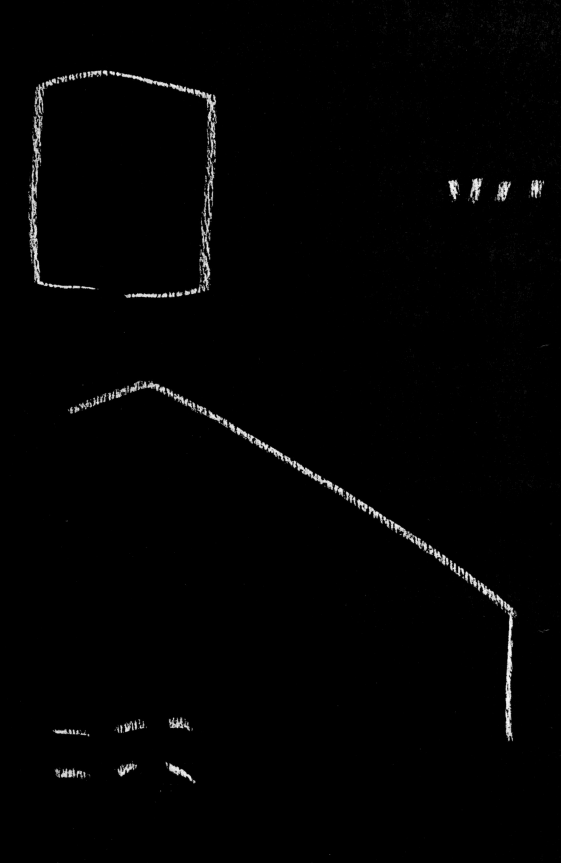

The NOISE of the RAIN
Collected Poems

Illustrations by

SARAH PLIMPTON

Sheep Meadow Press
Rhinebeck, New York

The Every Day was first published by the Pleasure Boat Studio in 2013.

Designed and typeset by The Sheep Meadow Press
Distributed by The University Press of New England

Front Cover: Sarah Plimpton

Library of Congress Cataloging-in-Publication Data

Names: Plimpton, Sarah, 1936- author.
Title: The noise of the rain / Sarah Plimpton.
Description: Rhinebeck, NY : Sheep Meadow Press, [2016]
Identifiers: LCCN 2016012599 | ISBN 9781937679682 (softcover)
Classification: LCC PS3566.L53 A6 2016 | DDC 811/.54--dc23
LC record available at https://lccn.loc.gov/2016012599

All inquiries and permission requests should be addressed to the publisher:

The Sheep Meadow Press
PO Box 84
Rhinebeck, NY 12514

Contents

THE EVERY DAY

THE NOISE OF THE RAIN

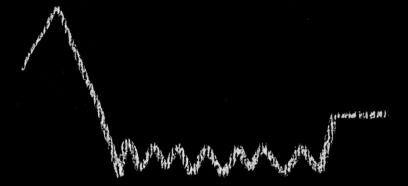

DAY TO DAY

I tried to open each day

wide at the door

but the sun had come through

at night

already shining

fitting into my head

where the sky broken

from the blue

beyond

and too far

that morning light

the dream you see

is the day to day

STORMS

open each day

now

to see

walking through

the wind

will slam

them shut

behind

THE NOISE OF THE RAIN

I waited by the window

the door that opens

darkens the room

the rain is from the outside

black strands of sky

tied with your fingers

folded to listen

standing

to whisper

the noise of the rain

A SCRAP OF LIGHT

a scrap of light

loose in the wind

blown away

caught in the grass

picking it up

one hand

would someone see?

running east

late in the day

straight from the sun

SMOKE

the sky has no top

in the blue and white

who would know

standing outside

taking the time

drifting up

smoke from a fire

is lost from sight

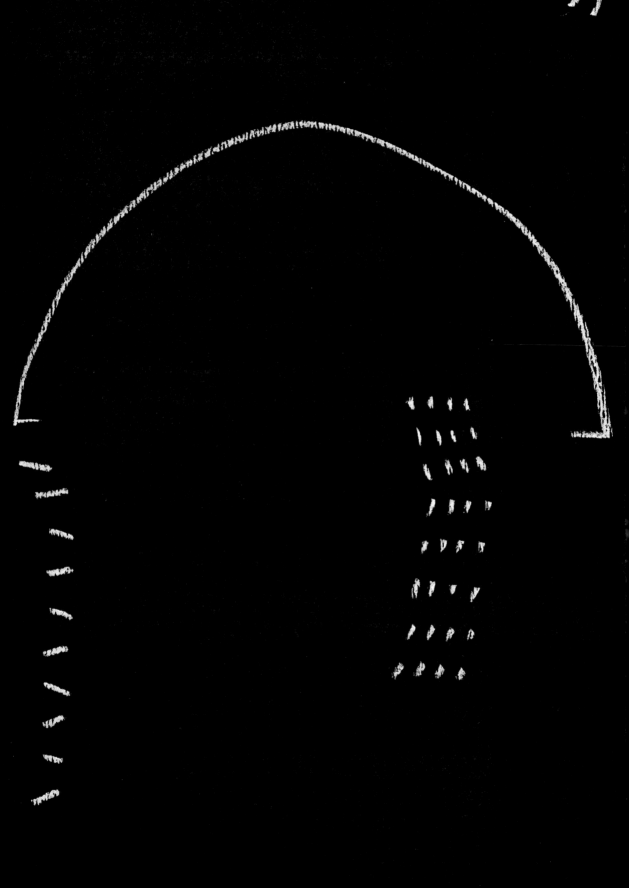

CHANGES IN THE WEATHER

you took the line

between the sky and the earth

and put it on the wall

painting it white

and waited for the weather to change

the clouds to come in

one by one

crowding in

dark curtains now

its now you said

the black rain

would come

all the way to the ground

painting out the line

you stepped back to look

and waited

and waited

for the weather to change

TIME TO SPARE

you shortened the time

cutting lengths of string

tied with bows

easy to pull

the end would do

DARK MATTER

one light out

and the stairs

are black

walking up to see

the night sky

where

the wind is down

a door

is cut to fit

the one step out

is beyond

your reach

STRINGS ON A SHADE

you were pulling

down the sky

strings on a shade

wound on your hand

black threads of tangled clouds

your folded smile

torn off at the edge

to leave behind

your feet walking in the dark

walking in the rain

further than I thought

SURVIVAL

I made holes to breathe

while running with feet overhead

the cold fingers were folded

to cut

answer now

those round holes

breathing out

one word and then

another

TEARS

I stepped out

in a wind

of slamming doors

loosened leaves

driving by

I don't have to wait

the rain runs on time

coming fast

black drops

to catch

my face

open eyes

TIME OUT

keep your hand open

to count the fingers

that is the hour

but each minute

opens

slits

wide like a knife

pouring out seconds

too fast to count

the running out

the up and down

too soon

it's now

the running out

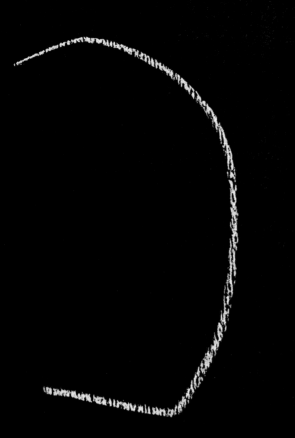

SHOUTS

the wind

cuts steps

to take

up and up

nowhere nowhere

shouts in the air

UP

if you walk up

keep both hands up

to hold the sky high

pushing the blue into the roof

cut the whisp of cloud

in two

for the brighter blue

you had not seen

THE WELL

the down too far

black as a well

shimmering

suddenly

dropping a stone

to listen

the far away

brightening

flattening out

when you look again

the circle of black

is already there

ONE MINUTE MORE

I had one minute more

but it was lost

along the way

I tried to count

with all the rest

the short and long

the dark and black

the bright and forgotten

I found the one

it was hanging loose

tying it all

a simple bow around the heart

one final pull

would let them go

OUT OF SIGHT

I put round clouds

on a blue sky

drawing them into

the walls of light

a wind picks up

pushing them just beyond

the noise comes later

whistling through in

the empty sky

PARTLY CLOUDY

blue steps cut into the hill

blue to count

up

blue you thought

taken up

but the light has patches

these sewn on clouds

are strung out ahead

THE SWING

swinging up

down

bend in

pushing out

high and higher

on the sky

touching each time

to leave a mark

against the blue

smudges of white

that disappear

swinging out

and sitting still

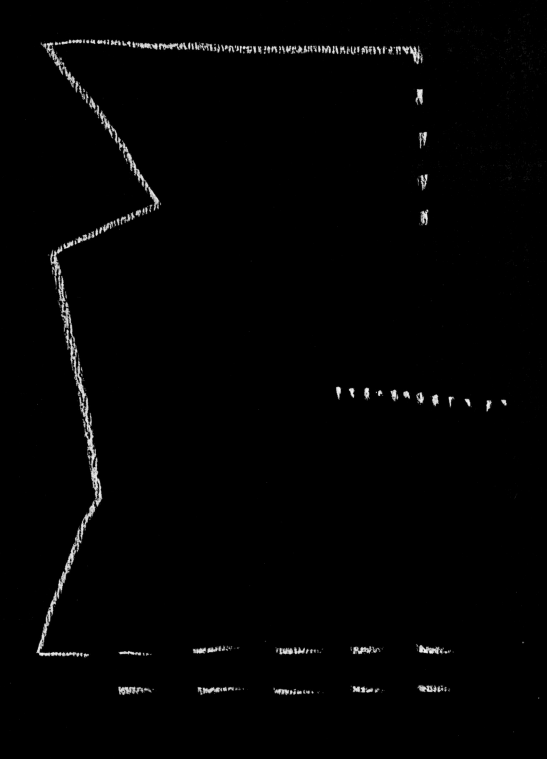

SURF

the wind is upside down

and underneath

ripping open water

white

foam of cracking light

twisting cold

slamming shut the noise

watching one by one

those broken waves

smoothing out

to disappear

running flat

and up the shore

VERTIGO

an eye bent

inside

held tight

a railing

on the edge of looking down

LANDSCAPE

a straight sun

cuts up and down

a door to open up

the outside green

stepping out

blue patches scatter the sky

the clouds are now and then

I'll tie them up

and walk away

it is another day

BLIND WORDS

the door left open

the sun lay flat

down on the floor

round and red

you cut out shapes

the scissors make

an angry edge

fiery letters

burn up the air

lost to the touch

devil may care

THE RAIN CAME AFTER

the wind turns over the leaves

to white

flashing on a white sky

ripping like flags

as fingers tear the cloth

shredded white

flecks of clouds

driven on

you couldn't hear

the rain came after

or the rain

that came before

MADE SMALL

you walked all the way

around the wind

making circles

of blue

cutting them smaller and smaller

until a mirror calm

spins out

skipping flat

to the end of the world

SUNSET

I drew a line around the sun

pulling tight

the paper red

cut for another sky

where the lonely clouds

stay still

and the wind has died

the colored air

breathed in and out

a day is painted in

and left to dry

GAMES

five minutes more

you said

holding back the cloud

small then

taking my time

walking on the ridge of light

balancing

the now and then

jump you said

now you said

the night would rise

stepping out

to jump the other way

FALL

I slipped a thought

a second too late

over and down

ice on your street

cracking an ankle

tight pain

like a drum

DEAD END

I walked too far

going on down behind

the sounds faded away

a moonless night

catches your shoulder

and pulls you around

steps are taken

with no way back

BLACK LIGHT

where the door is open

the sun makes a shadow

black on the outside

the box of light

is carried through

where the line of trees

leans to the south

over the road

we would walk to the end

counting in the dark

the left over stars

STEPPING ON COLOR

stepping on the color

blue

yesterday's sky

left in the street

left over clouds

gathering now

I am walking beyond

these are yesterday's shoes

A CLOUD TOOK THE SUN

a cloud took the sun

and put it away

a darkened room

cools quickly

make the time short

remember if you can

a hand on the door

is ready to go

COLD COLOR

when you ask directions

the blue wall is straight ahead

putting out a hand

to touch

drawing a fist full of air

one clear breath

the sharp cold color

disappearing

while you walk

always ahead

always asking

walking to the end

walking all the way around

the sharp cold color of the sky

THE COLOR RED

who did you ask?

before opening the door

walking

walking over there

steps on a road

it is the color you see

marked by the sun

the color red fired up

burning the wall

someone should ask

playing one note

again

again

the sun you see is red at the door

HORIZON

you spin the eye

and step

from black to grey

the sky to the sea

falling open

shining where you look

beginning to rain

FIVE

five times up

the sun over the sill

sharpened on its edge

the eye

cut to shine

mirrors of blue

fingers of blue

SOMEWHERE ELSE

caught in your eye

on an edge

hung

in the light

I couldn't see

staring out

the somewhere else

AS IF TO SEE

the eyes fasten in

the up and down

to remember

the blue and red skies

as you turn to ask

each step before

the answer shut

like a door in the wind

hours then

when I didn't know

the colors burn into the night

as if to see

as if I could see

DOUBLING BACK

a dark cloud

made the afternoon

turn back

running again

watching again

holding your breath

and

tying your hands in two

BLUE FROM AN EYE

you cut the window

into the sky

to stare

the bright sun

from today

would disappear

drawn red

to remember

but the blue

from an eye

would spread the light

and hide the stars

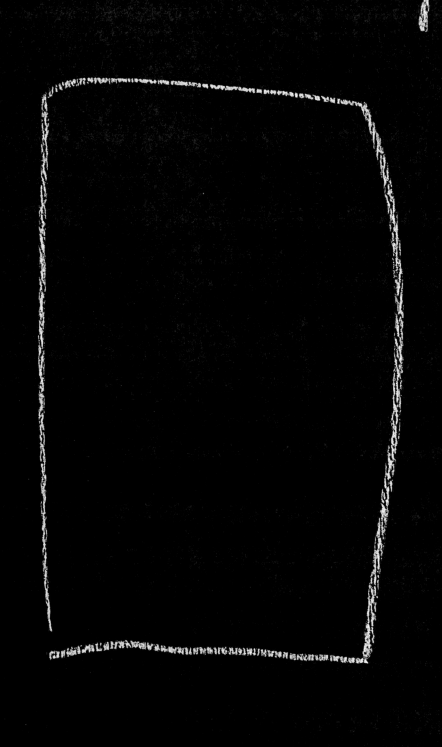

DOWNPOUR

the rain catches

on a warm night

bringing it down

the street is ahead

those flecks of light

from nowhere

disappear

COLD BLUE BREATH

cold blue breath

spirals out the

rotten wood

lungs close around the heart

eaten out

slanted light with

dimming shadows

the chest is up and down

each breath

puts one foot away

taking the other out

walk walk

the road is down hill

the moon will be up

STRANGE

looking sideways

into the light

small holes in the sky

an eye drills

the color through

BLUE COLOR

blue color like a flag

broken out

fresh the sun

all together

outside pages

cut out and pasted flat

I speak now

with color now

with hands on the sky

like the head

inside out

drawn out

the brighter air

to give away

to disappear

the light is fixed

and not from the eye

ONE TWO THREE

holding one eye

open

in the doorway

a bright wind

with a sharp edge

cuts holes

in the air

the faded sun

drains the breath

from green and red

watching the too fast light

running now

red to black

slamming shut

a one two three

HOLD ON

hold on

you said

to what?

this tree?

this cloudless sky?

this house?

hold with an eye

tighten the grip

this view?

this line of sight?

pull it in then

hand over hand

circles to coil

these pictures

of time and that time

for you?

for what?

it is never now

SHUT HANDS

the window came down

your shut hands

closed tight

the breath

the walking air

squeezed

red to hold

an evening sky

WHITE NIGHTS

swollen minutes

give more time

an endless day

counting your fingers

one to ten

once again

waiting for tomorrow

for the night

those black hours

open that package

found at the door

EARLY MORNING

walking out

and looking up

at the deathless clouds

with the words you meant to say

the red at the edges

is just beginning

before the sun

would

turn

the sky to white

DARK AFTERNOON

the trees have lost their leaves

black wet branches

below

sudden clouds

bare hands strip the sky

tie knots

with the wind

tears are moving fast

rain on the window

small drops of blood

run across the glass

COVER UP

the color painted on

blue air

breathed out

a sky so close

to touch

fingers on a wet surface

clouds

to cover up

the sun

CLEARING SKY

say yes

you took the smile

and put it up

from now on

a second face to add

a second sun

breaks the cloud

small pieces drift away

the clearing wind

CLOSING THE WINDOW

closing the window

is not what you thought

the light blows cold

painting the floor

black with stars

BLACK AIR

black gusts

of sudden air

black air

a cold breath

takes the lungs

takes the chill

close the door

when the room is dark

BLUE HOLES

small blue

holes

you looked inside

two at a time

transparent bone

BLINDED NOW

blind at the door

looking out

a yellow field of sun

a fixed smile

staring blind

I stepped against

the light

marking time

with the unseen day

you left behind

GIFT

any word

to wrap

the package

the color did not matter

inside was the night

with all the stars

a cold night, a gift

held without the moon

one present that

and not other

PAINTED IN

a day is painted in

the so many colors

numbered

one to five

and on and on

while the light

can last

counting up the seconds left

looking now

remembered

now or not at all

NAILED SHUT

the blue wall of stairs

to climb the sky

the straight up clouds

broken off at the top

standing to wait

for the last light

burned out black

to carry down

nailed shut

as a box of cold

put down once

and buried underground

PARADOX

keep your time

don't ask for mine

rolled up for later

those faster minutes

come and go

no waiting now

I'll keep my

secrets close at hand

THE EVERY DAY

THE EVERY DAY

twisted into the sky

with your hands

I'd never seen that blue before

wrung out with

the paper walls

of air

until the rain

soaked through

a smaller patch behind the grey

I'd remember once

and then again

like the sun

the every day

THE OTHER SUN

a sudden light

but then you had already gone

the eye is so straight

looking behind

a door to shut

and open

I had forgotten to ask

looking only once

the whole sky

was there

that bright blue

as if painted in

the other sun

EVERY STEP

I would take your voice uphill

in the heat

I had not remembered the sun

something had to break

when you cry again and again

your head against the sky

beaten

in

to light

the night

is just as close

WHEREVER

the eyes narrowing

in the door

round mouths of light

that shut

the air

between the cracks

of blue

small windows

cut in the

winters head

open upside down

the ground

SURFACE

I stumbled

from the height

and fell

against the sky

broken from the edge

the cliff

black against

the stars

falling from underneath

the ground had

disappeared

SMALL HANDS

the mountain shades in the sun

blue

pockets of air

small hands

around the eye

the first green

printed

almost flat

the earth

KNOTS

the light

twisted

in

the head

knotted

behind the eye

its rough edge

catches on the sun

the blue sea of air

BURNT VISION

the night in the head

burning holes

to the sky

stars on the edge

the charred wall

hollowed out

the face

from the sun

SPLIT ROUND

a larger face

the sky

lying open

in the road

split

round at the back

the blue earth

of stones

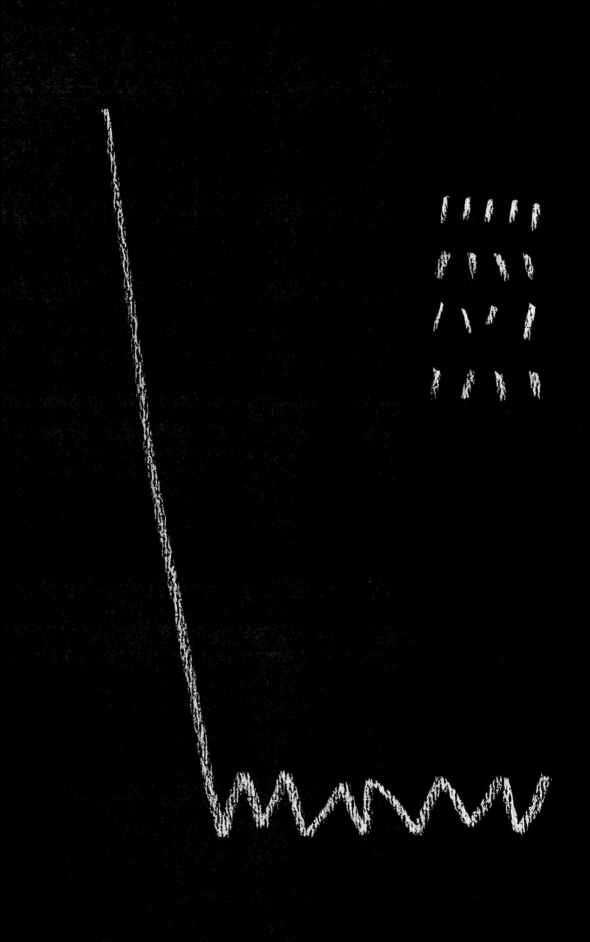

BURIAL

that bright edge of sky

lined

a solid face

packed in bones

a buried earth

drying flat

on the sheets of stone

EDGES

an eye of broken glass

the sky on its edge

at the top of the wall

the bright line of the day

splintered

from the sun

and already dark

YOUR COLOR

I'd drawn the light into the face

as if quickly

to watch the whole sky once

when I think of color

putting it on here and there

 yours

as if the mountain were yours

fast in the blue

but brighter

the sun

when it is suddenly cold

BLACK FOR WHITE

the black I couldn't see

your hand from the page

outlines the ink

the night

its face

opened in white

a light is broken

in the back

the sharp edge

crosses the eye

the window is on a hinge

turning the night

to the other side

UNDERNEATH

the windows cut

into the road

down to the sky

the earth

from underneath

the night traveling

already shut

catching white

against

the clouds

THIN EDGE

the day stretched too thin

tearing off

to see

an eye you hadn't closed

the light would disappear

pulled so tight with

the breath

I held too long

shall I go to look

where the broken blue

has turned to

night

TALKING

you talked so fast

I hadn't thought

to walk

and the feet

are always first

carried like children

running so fast

the door is open

green

like the white of the sun

to ask

when I couldn't speak

is it to remember

you had already left

QUESTIONS

I asked again

but it is not what I said

was it the sun that

you made

but the sky has bits of cloud

I'd straighten up with color

working from the blue

the light

to touch

like the air

I talk to listen

like the questions

of a child

you had

already known

ROAD MAP

the sun is straight ahead

I would see to walk

but there is no color

to take out

as bones from

a box

the eye is from the road

and the world is no longer round

BREATH

I opened the door

only once

with an eye to stand behind

the light

driven up

until the sky

was out of sight

the air is cut out

to see

the color black

I was walking so fast

there was

no place

to breathe

BLUE INTRUSION

the eyes

cut through

looking out

such mirrors

of the sky

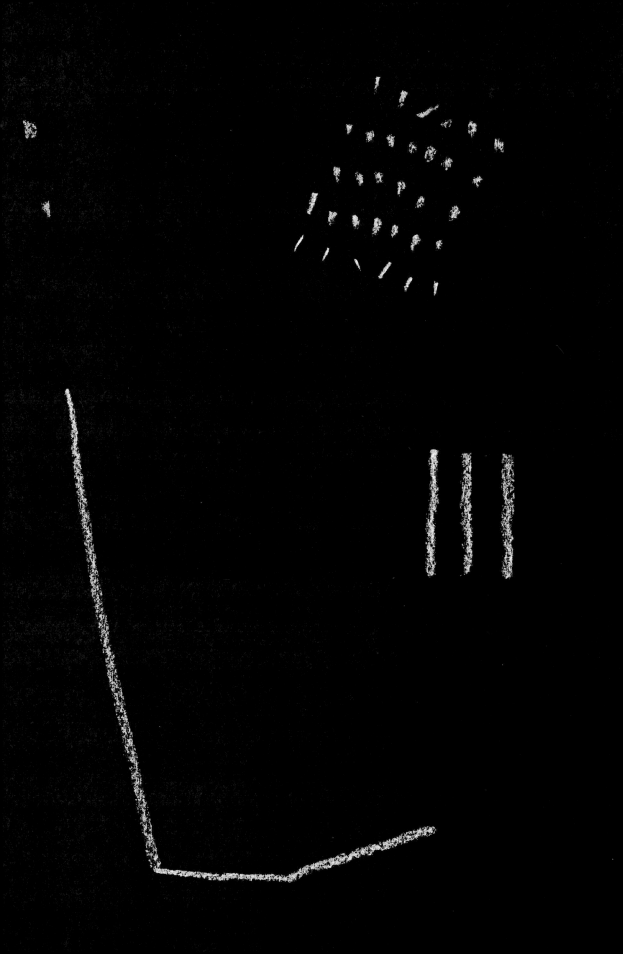

WALKING

the flowers you like are on the side of the road

a drift of light

is piling up across the eye

my hands are shined again

and again

throwing them out to catch

the air

but I had forgotten that walking

takes such time

and when I looked around

the road had turned

and was

straight uphill

BLUE IN AN INSTANT

where the blue in an instant

lifts the sun

out

I would laugh

catching

catching up

the light is just behind

from hand to hand

always to remember

the color you said

where the sky is drawn

the face

put down like tears

as white is the half

to cover the ground

AGAIN AND AGAIN

the light is to fold

again and again

packed to remember

the eye

you would know

as if inside out

and all the world

but I will put the color in

like the sky from the sun

as if I never had a name

BOX FOR AN EYE

the smaller sky

from the head

built over

the sun

the clouds

in the blue air

blocked into light

the eye fastened

into the bone

the earth underneath

DRIFTING

I floated out from the light

holding up as sleep

the dream

so short

from the boat

reaching over

for the stars

down through the water

spots of light

that reflect

in the cold

HOURS TO DAYS

I took the sky by the edge

lifting the color

the red for evening

and drew a line

into the black

a road from the map

yours

to take

the stars are first

with hours to days

did you think I could see

the place for an eye

it is only the night

spread already

face up

with cold

CRACKS IN THE FLOOR

I kicked up the light

as if cracks in the floor

like the earth

walking over and over

to look

where the night has fallen

through

disappeared with its stars

down

the color down

as if the sun

behind the eye

WALL OF STARS

not that I quite want to hold the light

the hands are

built in

and the window broken at the side

the face is from the ground

its dark holes

center

the night in a dark

wall of stars

BURIED FIELDS

the face is broken

open at the sky

and looking in

to see the stars

unwind

the light is down hill

holding to the curve

I run at the road

cutting across

those buried fields

of sight

FORGOTTEN

I had turned around

with every eye

I had thought

I had

the ground had touched the sky

that was where you stepped

in that light

I could remember

but if you talk

it is as if

there isn't the face

and the rain would clear

I had walked too far

forgetting where

the words are underneath

each step

like its muscle

and then they disappear

ONLY NOW

when you can't make the sun

again

to see

the sky put on its shoulders of blue

the eye is straight ahead

just in front the road

dug up and buried already

the light can be black

and shining

if crows can be golden

my head is outside

its room

its weight

in my hands set down

forgotten

it is the black

I will remember

once

and then again

ATELIER

the light is

thick with paint

I put the sun across the room

picking up the blue

an hour for the cold

when I didn't think to ask

every hour

and then the day

to see

occasionally

a sky

and then the clouds

marked in a

brightness

I hadn't seen

opening the window

you had painted in

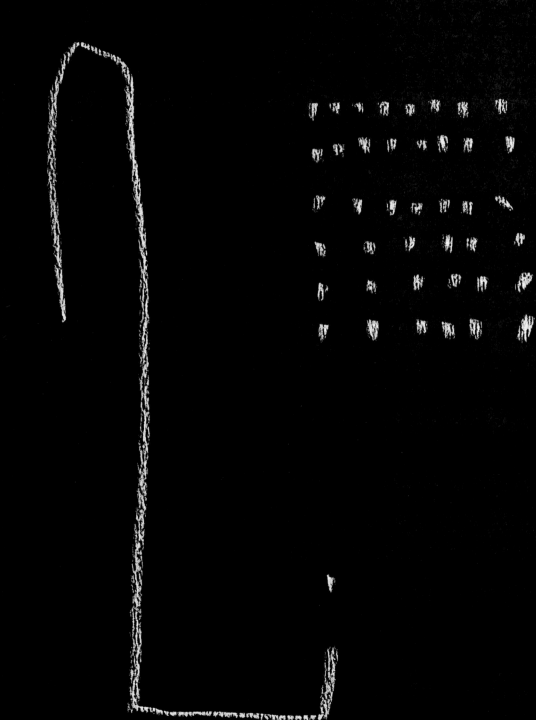

SIDEWAYS TO SEE

I walked for the sun

but the breath breaks

like the step up

sticking to the air

the brightness would burn

away

outside

I stopped to wait

sideways now

across the road

the eye

or none

the cold in and out

laying the head flat

as the sky across the page

for the night

to move

I'll have its light

to color in

CORNFLOWERS

I would hold the face

up to the light

looking through

to the air

a blue haze of flowers

picking up those

pieces of sky

the color of tears

BACKWARDS

which face is taken inside

is it just to see

and not to cry

with eyes like the earth

the cleared air

there are clouds from the rain

the road is so short

and walking to the end

the sun would disappear

the night is from the night before

CLOSE VISION

then what is your face?

I could see the eyes

gathered tight

blue

but then

close vision

is only the air

shining white sheets

of sky

GROUNDED

the door is open

like the night outside

I'll stand to walk

as if the roads

are already paved

but the stars

are underneath

REFRACTION

the blue crack

in the rain

widens through the head

filling

out with sky

drawn at the

edge

an eye

at the line of air

where the light

bends

through the tears

NOW AND THEN

each star is now

and then

I'll count

and every breath

the words can be color

but the eye

has drained its tears

I emptied the rest

even the name

looking out

once more

it wasn't there

the night had no sky

turning inside out the face

to laugh

to roughen the wind

the empty holes

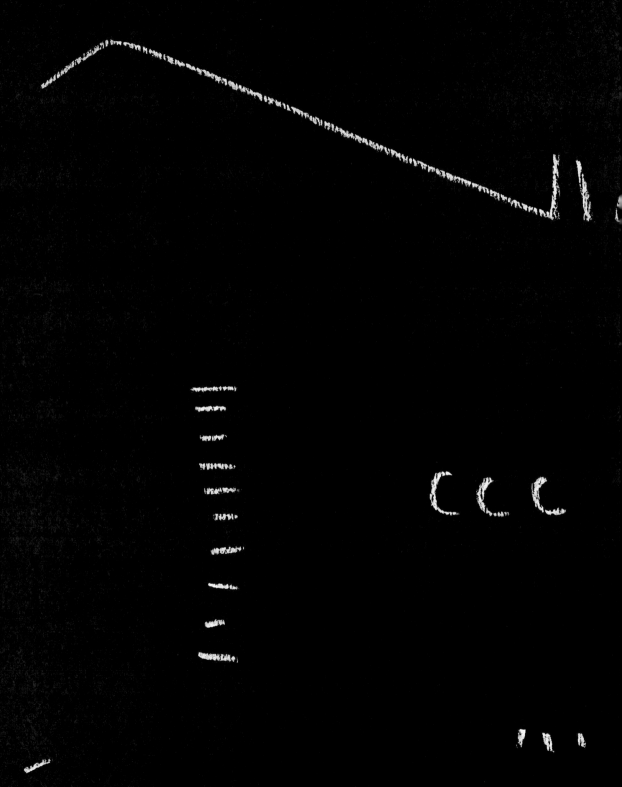

PRESSURE

the sky forced out

with the air

a breath gone

from the dark face

the ground dug up

around the eye

opened and closed

the round hole of light

blackened outside

and squeezed from

the hand

YOU

have you taken

the air

the room is empty

where you sat

the chair is moved to the window

how do you look behind?

is that the door?

the sky

has such

light

without

the sun

THE BLUE FACE

the blue face

and the night is off the sky

looking and not to see

the mouth is lying open

only the skin and bone

to touch

the stillness takes the cold

the cross

from the road

STRAIGHT EDGE

the sky held again

the speed

I could run where

your hands had put those bits of blue

along the road

the light will follow

down behind the earth

when the heart is opened inside out

each hour has

its straightened edge of black

PATCHES

I'll put the sky

up to the light

but the sun

is traced in black

and that page

was turned

the night

has its shadows

patched with rain

EDGES ARE STEPS

the curtain has its stars

you wouldn't hear

and the light I lit

has gone

the edges

are steps

with the night instead

OUTSIDE

your window is from the night

are those eyes to see?

and mine?

I hadn't looked

the sky was too close

with its sun at the edge

but the color is black

when you open the face

and the door

is to step outside

WHAT SUN?

what sun

so close

to break

the sky

burning off the blue

from the night

behind

the face

the dawn outside

brightening through the holes

strung through the head

the grasses thinner in the wind

pulled in the gate

standing in the shadows

the walls of the sun

PULLING THE FACE OFF THE BONE

you pulled the face

off the bone

holding your arms high

enough

as the night

spreads up

the steps are all the way

to the sky

when I turned to speak

as if the air

had gone

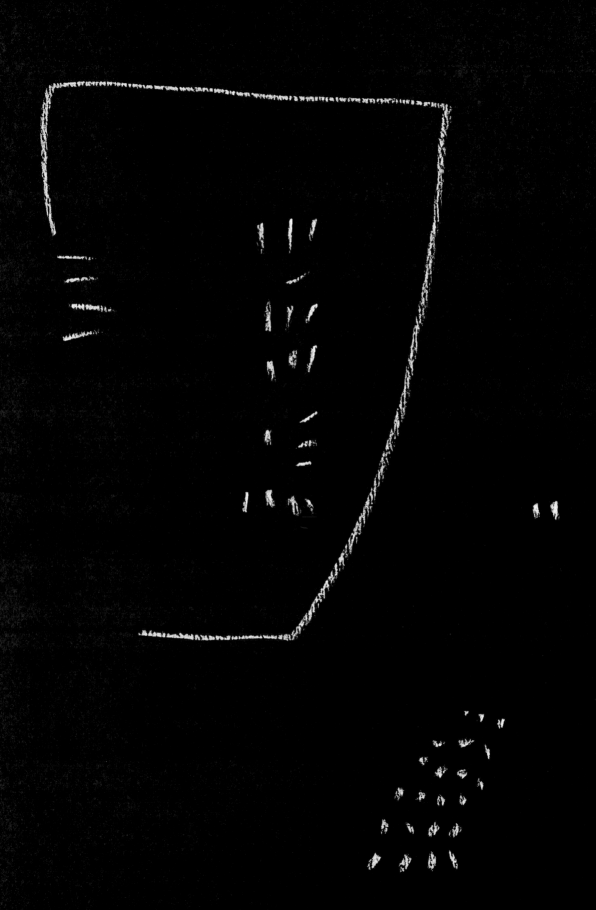

THE SUN IN THE ROAD

is there just the sky

to watch

I'll turn to look for

the sun in the road

but the view is gone

I'll talk again

to hear

the air is tightened

and the light is from there to there

is it where you are

mine is just the heart

and standing up to breathe

your face is broken into light

and the night is on the other side

painted in across the eye

the black sky

holds its stars

like dust

A SHORTENED SKY

a shortened sky

your sun

straight down

cutting edges on the broken light

open up along my eye

the fields inside

laid out flat

transparent

in the air

the head inside a

solid sky

IVORY BLACK

I'll color in the sky

at night

ivory black

made like an eye

to watch

an inside face

a wall of sky

can be cut into stars

but the sun is out of reach

tearing down the road is twice as fast

I could never double back

to see

the day

begin

the paint had dried

before the end

INSIDE OUT

you opened the door

but the face was at the night

you would see the stars

when you turn to leave

the small earth

you dug up

is buried again

tied up in its knot and

the sky was left inside

BLUE ON BLUE

I had taken that sky down

to put away

clouds and rain

the sun underneath

as if tears could be undone

the blue is spread on the ground

where you walked

the cornflowers you said

there and there

picking the sky

to put in my hand

that day

that one day

as fast as it went

blue on

blue

to choose

BLACK AS IF THE HEIGHT

black as if the height

stands in minutes

looking down to tell the time

over and over

calling the hours

the steps are split like an eye in two

taken down

the white into black

spreading stars

falling away

to make the sky

I would never see

WEATHER

the sun rubbed thin

across the eye

the shadows from the head

straighten into rain

the sky clears behind

empty rooms

of blue

DUSK

the new moon

slips inside

a thin smile

I put the hour up on end

cracked round

your voice that comes apart

AS IF NOTHING COULD BE SAID

you asked a question

about the weather

I'll look outside

and watch the rain

a day goes by

poured out

water from the glass

as if nothing could be said

JUST NOW

the light is to catch

the color

blue like an eye

standing at the door

the sky was only once

and then again

where you walked

the garden has its roses

just in bloom

BLACK PALETTE

I tied the eyes together

and mixed the colors

black

the sun burned through

to see

never seen

enough

the night to paint

and flattened out across the ground

TOMORROW

it cleared

after the rain

the late afternoon

the light

all at once

shining off the leaves

gathered in

untied

I took it

to save

sharpening the face to the wind

not to ask anymore

the light

that was yours

HALF DAY

an hour made up

drawn in black

lines of clouds

folded back and forth

over the sky

staring underneath

the time packed

and sent away

sitting down to wait

STRAIGHT UP

the smile faces up

catching the light

an hour to stop

listening and the wind

changes overhead

the clouds move in

one for another

blind when I looked

and not to the sky

I'd forgotten

to count

WORDS

I was woken up

on the road

lying on words

like stones

at the edge

the whole sky

turned upside down

the clouds are pushing to the side

their same color

has its taste

spoken out

like those words

I would hear

pressed to the hand

and sharpened

to a fist

FIRES

I caught your face on fire

the room too small

to breathe

the too much light

to see

to put it out

as if the sun

and made without

FUSION

a smile to have

made

even as the sky shines

seen

while the sun

burns its wood

from the flame

FIELD FLOWERS

just there

in front

where you spoke

and to wait

the air stands

to one side

flowers in a room

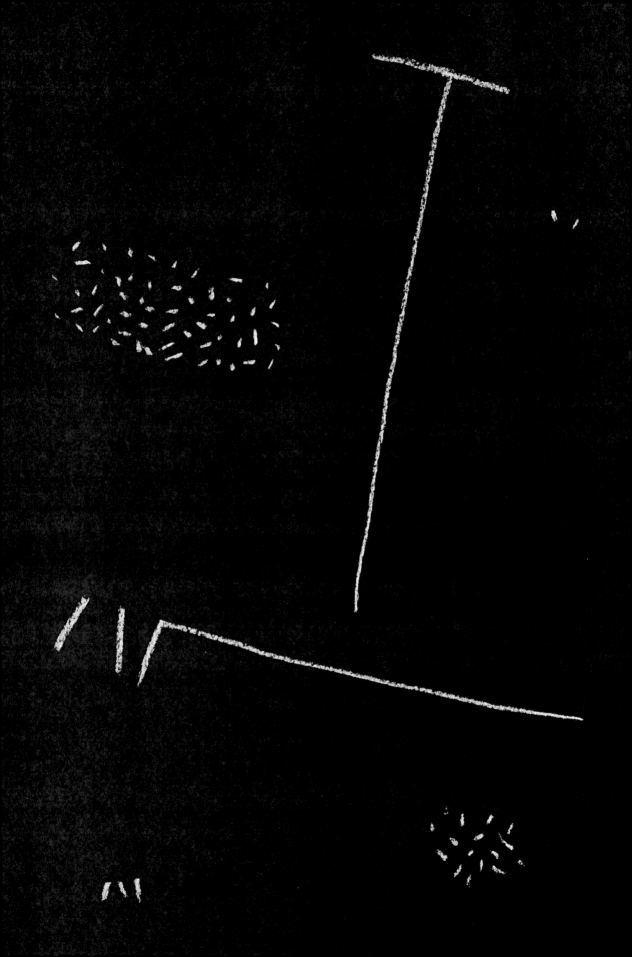

PAINT

I painted out the sky

thickening the paint

white like the sun

covering over

an eye

one then the other

patches of light

to spread

like a smile

AFTERNOON

you made the smile

folded into a small package

put down on the table

to keep

we marched together

there was no wind

only the road

going along

the clouds are like smoke

with the fire behind

SUDDEN WORDS

forced colors

spoken out of turn

flowers in the room

a hand on the door

opened too soon

SPILLED LIGHT

I spilled the light

onto the floor

blinded underfoot

walking away

I held out a hand

black fingers

are stripes

along the wall

DICE

a head shaken

the words like dice

thrown out

stones on the road

to stub your toe

FLARES

you left the color behind

red flowers on the table

holes in the sky

shaped to burn

.

VISITS

visited

you bent a smile into the mouth

the same smile

muscles in place

forced

as a stick that opens

the teeth

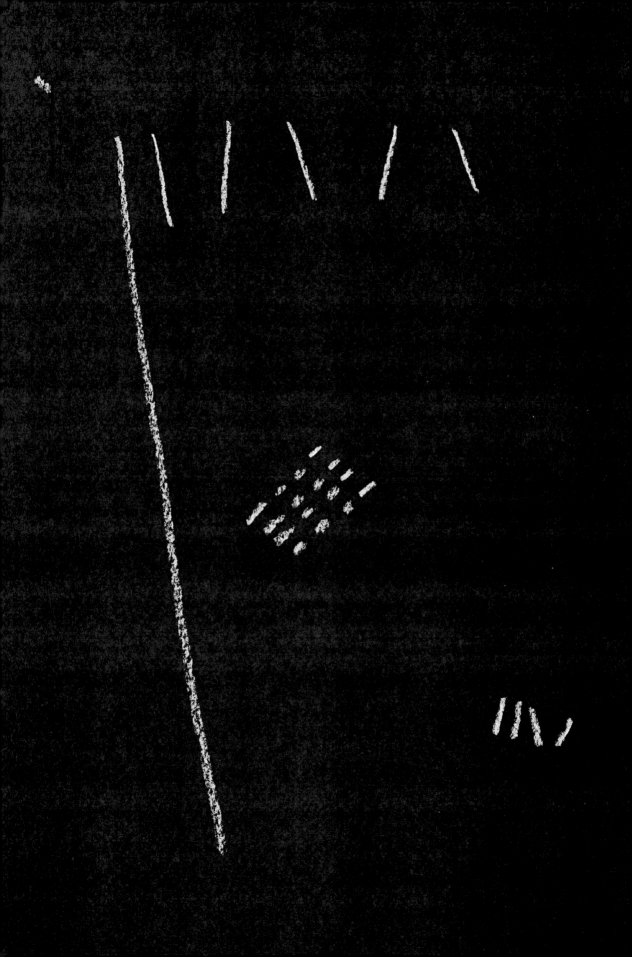

AJAR

I'll laugh

catching on the air

the hands to let go

the breath

and the hours

while the afternoon

is outside

with the sun

spun out

the dark is left open

like the door to leave

A SKY IS DOWN

you sit straight

when the sky is down

black lines of blue cold

drawn

the hours turn your hands

seconds to count

and nothing to remember

OUTSIDE

I took one eye off

then a step

to run out onto the night

breathing inside out

cold air

from the lungs

MASKS

you took out your face

and put it down

the mouth opens

its round circle

black in the air

moving in and out

hung in the center

and suddenly still

BLUE AND BLACK

overtaken

on the road

clouds from behind

pulled along

the wind

blue and black

driven on

DAYS

one day and another

outside

to look

the child jumps in and out

the door

trying the air

the clouds will build

dark blue

pushed under

where the sun splits

an hour off

the words to listen

then to forget

standing still

the earth brought up

to bury the cold

lowering one day

into the next

AUTHOR BIOGRAPHY

Sarah Plimpton is a painter, poet, and novelist. Her novel, *Hurry Along*, was published by Pleasure Boat Studio. Her poems and prose have appeared in *The New York of Books*, *The Paris Review*, and the *Denver Quarterly* among other magazines. A collection of her poems is translated into French, *L'Autre Soleil*, published by Le Cormier, Belgium. Her work may be found in various museum and library collections including the Whitney Museum of American Art, the Museum of Fine Arts, Boston, and the Metropolitan Museum of Art. She divides her time between New York City and France.